INHER
HELL

A £4.2 MILLION FRAUD

TOM RENNY

Editing, design, typesetting and publishing by UK Book Publishing

www.ukbookpublishing.com

ISBN: 978-1-917329-32-3

INHERITANCE HELL

A £4.2 MILLION FRAUD

FOREWORD

If you'd asked me a few years ago, I never would have believed I would be writing this account. I am no expert in law, inheritance or probate. However, when I was left a 5% portion of inheritance, I found myself plunged into a high-profile court case; the developments of which almost seemed fictional.

I wanted to write this account to raise awareness of the flaws of probate in the UK. What happened to me could easily happen to others if the law isn't changed around probate and inheritance. We followed all the procedures, yet still found ourselves fighting a legal case – and it still baffles me to this day as to how it ever got this far. With little evidence, the will I was due to inherit under was legally challenged and I still can't quite understand how it was able to progress as far as it did. If something like this happened to me, it could easily happen to you – even if you followed the correct procedures in this country as we did.

Another reason I chose to write was for the attention it would help bring to our case. Traditionally, I have been brought up in a family where I was taught from an early age to keep financial and personal matters to myself. Added to this, I am naturally a private person and dislike social media and the attention it draws. Why, you might ask then, am I writing about and going public with my story? Initially, I didn't have a choice. As you will learn, I found the case plastered across the front pages of national newspapers without any prior warning. You will read in the following chapters that this came as a huge shock. So, in terms of attracting public attention, I didn't really have a say. Also, as the case took its twists and turns, I began to see the benefits that the public attention might bring. If I was to go about trying to change the law and procedures in this country, then I would need to raise awareness and public attention in order to start making changes to our legal system. The only way to bring about change is by making more people aware of the flaws in our system. Hopefully, our case can serve as an example.

After the case went public, I found myself reading the many comments on the articles and realised how much public interest this generated. I was also being asked about it by close friends and family who had stumbled upon the article and hadn't realised what I was embroiled in. If it gained so much interest, then surely it was a story people would want to read. Even if this story doesn't change the law, at least it has raised awareness.

Finally, writing this has acted as a form of therapy for me throughout the case. I have always enjoyed writing and when I became a qualified teacher, I began to write some of my own teaching resources; I have even published short stories with comprehension questions for 7–11-year-olds. As the months rumbled on and the case kept taking different directions, writing all of this down has helped me process the ordeal.

I hope my story gives an insight into the problems in our legal system and will inspire you to support my campaign to change the law around this.

I have separated this account into several chapters based on significant events, with the titles highlighting time periods covered. Some chapters last months, others weeks, and the trial at the end lasting days.

As a final note, I would like to emphasise that this book has been told solely from my perspective and experience. This story is my own. I have tried my very best to omit the views and opinions of the other beneficiaries and their experiences, and have consciously left out their specific names. Although a shared, public case, I wanted to be as accurate to my feelings and experiences as I saw them. I have tried my utmost to keep the personal opinions of beneficiaries, solicitors and anyone else involved in the case out of this book. I hope that by doing this, you will find this account a true reflection of my experience.

This is my story of how the initially exciting news became one of the most traumatic and difficult experiences of my life.

LITTLE MORE THAN A NAME

EARLY 2020

I could probably count the number of interactions I had with Maureen Renny on one hand. To be honest, she was really nothing more than a name to me. I could technically call her my "Step-Grandmother" as she had married my paternal grandfather long before I was born, following the very premature death of my grandmother. But the only occasions I had ever met Maureen in person was at the hospital in 1999 and 2000 when I was taken to visit my dying paternal grandfather. I was only eight years old at the time and so my memory of her and my grandfather is very limited. All I can really remember of those visits was my grandfather smiling at me from his hospital bed as I showed him the new Star Wars action figures that he had bought me for my birthday (of which I still have to this day). I still find it quite sad that the only memory I have of him is in a hospital bed, hooked up to a machine.

As an eight-year-old, I was too young to question or even understand why it was that I was meeting my grandfather for the first time in hospital. My father had a fractured relationship with his stepmother and so our contact was extremely limited. However, this is another story entirely and not one I feel is my place to tell.

In the subsequent years after my grandfather's passing, I had barely any contact from Maureen. I never saw her in person again. The only interaction was indirectly through my mum who kept in contact with Maureen by sending school photos and updates about me and my sister as well as one of her annual Christmas letters, which she would post to various distant relatives and friends, summing up the year for our family and any notable events that had occurred that year. I can't say I ever looked at or read any of these letters and can't remember having any desire to either (I was a typical disinterested teenage boy at the time). So, if you were hoping to hear any riveting details of our family days out and significant birthdays, I'm afraid you will be disappointed!

The first significant contact we had from Maureen came many years later in 2016 when I was 23 years old. It was a couple of years after I had graduated from Newcastle University and I was just venturing out into the working world. I had enjoyed life in Newcastle and loved the region so much that I decided to stay there after graduating. I had also met my now-wife whilst studying at university and, in 2016, we were renting a house together. I grew up in Essex and in 2016 my parents were still living there so were at the other end of the country. One day, I received a phone call from my mum who told me that she had had a call from one of Maureen's carers. The carer had rung to ask for the full names, addresses and dates of birth of both my sister and myself on Maureen's behalf. Maureen wasn't communicating herself, but my mum could hear her instructing the carer in the background. It was apparent from this that Maureen's health was declining (an important point to highlight now as it becomes significant later on). For what reason Maureen wanted our personal information for, she didn't say, but my mum strongly suspected it had something to do with her will and inheritance. What else could she possibly want to know this for? That's what my mum surmised anyway. She hadn't gone into any further detail and we heard no more after that.

The next point of contact came two years later in August 2018 when I got married. To my great surprise, I received a wedding card from Maureen containing a monetary gift. She would have found out about my wedding from my mum's annual Christmas letter. Although her signature was at the bottom, I could tell that the remainder of the card had been written on her behalf. It was apparent that her health was continuing to deteriorate. I still have the card today alongside our other wedding cards to remember our special day. I hadn't expected any gift from her at all, let alone contact, and I must admit, it had come as a great surprise. As with all the other wedding gifts we received, we sent a thank you letter to Maureen with a photo of my wife and I on our wedding day. I didn't expect her to reply and unsurprisingly, I received no response. After that, I never heard anything more of her until a couple of years later when I was informed of her passing.

The first I heard of Maureen's death was from my mum who sent me a text message the morning after Maureen died, just before I was due to start work back in January 2020. To say I felt any sort of emotion would be completely untrue. As I said previously, she was really no more than a name to me. Mum told me that I might possibly hear something from the solicitors once the probate came through but, as was typical of my mum, she instructed me not to get my hopes up. We didn't know for certain whether my sister and I had been included in any inheritance and if we had, it might be nothing more than just a token gift and nothing of significance. "Just assume you might be getting £20," Mum told me. "You might not even get that." Obviously, I would be lying if I told you I didn't get my hopes up slightly. After all, why else would Maureen have rung up asking for our information a few years earlier? Maureen had no children of her own. Moreover, I knew Maureen had also been distinctly aware that my sister and I were the only grandchildren of her deceased husband. Could it be that she felt duty-bound to include us in the inheritance? These questions rattled through my head over the following days, but eventually I put it to the back of my mind. I would hear when it was time, and it would probably be nothing exciting.

I didn't realise how wrong I would be. Little did I know what was about to unfold over the next few years. Soon, hope would be very quickly replaced by despair and frustration as Maureen's will would end up gaining so much attention it would make the front page of newspapers and even end up in Crown Court. It all began with a woman named Leigh Voysey.

INHERITANCE AND DISPUTE

MARCH 2020-MARCH 2022

To hear that my sister and I had each been left 5% of the estate when probate came through in Spring 2020 was exciting news for both of us. Initially, we didn't know how much we were going to receive. We were aware of Hill House, which Maureen and my grandfather had owned in Much Hadham, Hertfordshire, and where Maureen had still been living when she passed. This was a huge seven-bed home which was referred to locally as "The Barn School", owing to its previous usage as a private school. Maureen had also served as its headmistress in the past. However, we weren't aware of the large property portfolio that my grandfather and Maureen had built up over the years and we learnt that Maureen had also owned a number of properties across the country which made up the total estate. This portfolio ranged from a flat in London to a property on the South Coast. In terms of a specific figure, we would have to wait until all the properties sold before we would know how much this 5% would actually be worth. It would clearly be a sizeable amount, but for the moment, I could only make an educated guess based on the property valuations.

At this point, I was in my late 20s and had been working as a Primary School Teacher for a number of years. My parents had diligently made sure that I had saved money during my childhood in order that I would be able to afford a house deposit when I grew up. My mum has always been, and continues to be, very astute when it comes to money and I'm sure she was preparing for my future from the moment I was born. This had involved tucking nearly all my birthday and Christmas money aside each year. Unsurprisingly, as a child I had been unhappy with this arrangement, but it is something I am very grateful for now as it allowed me to get on the housing ladder much earlier than a lot of my peers. It was one of the wisest life choices my parents made for me and was crucial for me buying my first house. So, at this point in time, although not wealthy, I did consider myself to be in a fortunate position.

However, the inheritance would potentially allow me to move to a bigger house; and when the properties had all sold and the inheritance began to come through in the Spring of 2021, this is exactly what my wife and I used the money to do. It was a nice amount of money which I had never had before and I felt we used it wisely. I was extremely grateful for what I had received at this stage of my life and we told only our closest friends and family about the inheritance. I was consciously aware that many of my peers were desperate to get on the housing ladder and I didn't want to mention anything as it may have come across like I was bragging. I felt incredibly lucky to have received such an amount and didn't want it being common knowledge. I thought that was the end of the matter; I had no idea what was about to unfold in the following months.

By May 2021 we were settled in our new home. I was due one more instalment from the inheritance which I planned to use on some home improvements before tucking any remainder aside for a rainy day. This was when things began to take a twist. The first clue that something was not quite right was when I suddenly had no contact from the solicitors who were distributing the estate. Up until this point, I was being kept regularly updated regarding the estate and its distribution. Suddenly, this contact stopped altogether. At first, I assumed the solicitors must be busy and there was just some delay to the final distribution. Eventually, they did get back to me and this is when the shocking news came through.

It emerged that one morning, a woman named Leigh Voysey had appeared at the solicitors in Hertfordshire claiming that she had a will from Maureen Renny dated from September 2019, which left the entire estate to her. When questioned further, Leigh claimed that one evening, after the carers had left Maureen, she and her witnesses (both close acquaintances of hers) arrived at Hill House to sign this new will at Maureen's instruction. This was the September before her passing (she died in the following January). Allegedly, this new will had been sitting at the table for them to sign, and Leigh stated Maureen had wanted this will kept secret from everyone else, including her carers. Leigh had been a carer for

Maureen on one occasion back in 2016 and had also known Maureen from her time as a headteacher when Leigh had attended the Barn School as a pupil. As to her coming forward more than a year after Maureen had died, Leigh stated she had been too unwell over the previous year to come forward and that was why we were only hearing about this new will now.

In her communication, Leigh Voysey claimed that she had visited Maureen secretly at Maureen's behest. According to Leigh Voysey, Maureen hadn't wanted Hill House sold to developers and so had left it to Leigh in order to prevent such a sale. Leigh stated Maureen had asked for this new will to be drawn up in secret, not only to prevent Hill House and the land being sold to developers, but also because Maureen thought it would be highly amusing to sideline the beneficiaries of the 2016 will. Furthermore, Leigh Voysey presented a piece of jewellery saying that Maureen had given this to Leigh's daughter as a gift before she died and this somehow proved that her claim was legitimate. I want to emphasise there was no letter or receipt attached to this piece of jewellery which linked its purchase to Maureen. It was purely what Leigh presented in her belief that it added evidence to her claims.

Obviously, I had a lot of questions. Firstly, who was this woman and why had she only come forward now when Maureen had died nearly a year and a half previously, despite claiming she had been ill for the past year? What had really taken her so long? Even if she was ill, how could it possibly have taken more than a year to come forward?

Added to this, why would Maureen leave everything to this one woman who was of no relation to her and had been a carer for Maureen on just *one* occasion? Furthermore, Maureen had left a large percentage of the estate to various charities in the 2016 will, so I was more than a little doubtful as to Leigh's claim. The whole situation baffled me and had come out of nowhere. The more I thought about it, the more suspicious I became; shock had been replaced by cynicism. I began to suspect Leigh Voysey had only known about the inheritance and Maureen's passing when she saw that Hill House had been sold around a similar time, particularly as it later came to light that she had first visited the house's Estate Agents prior to appearing at our solicitors. I couldn't help but connect this with her sudden arrival. I strongly felt she had seen the value of the house and had been driven by greed. Moreover, the only people who were supporting Leigh's claims were her father and her partner who I felt were flawed witnesses as both were close family members who would have a vested interest in Leigh's claims. I knew from experience that important documents such as passports and driving licences would need signatures from professional witnesses who weren't familial ties with vested interests. So, it is unsurprising to say that from the offset, I was sceptical.

It appeared that my scepticism was shared by our solicitors who had been communicating with Leigh on our behalf through various letters, urging her to step aside. What evidence did she have that could possibly entitle her to the inheritance and why was it only now she was coming forward to claim the estate? Despite numerous attempts to persuade her to desist, Leigh would not step aside. I already feared where this was all heading. Suddenly, the inheritance, which started as a gift, was hurtling towards a full-blown court case.

There were many reasons why I believed Leigh Voysey was lying and that her claims also made the solicitors and all the beneficiaries distrust her claim. Firstly, in the 2019 will that Leigh Voysey had come forward with, there was no reference to any of the other properties and Leigh Voysey seemed to have no knowledge of these whatsoever. As mentioned, Maureen had owned a number of properties in addition to Hill House across the country which were included in the estate. Leigh's 2019 will only made mention of Hill House and she clearly had no idea Maureen owned other properties. Surely, if this was a new will from Maureen, the other properties would have been included? It was as if they didn't exist. Additionally, Maureen had left a large proportion of the inheritance to several charities and institutions. There was no mention of this in the 2019 will; according to Leigh, everything had been left to her. Suddenly, all these charitable organisations had also been cut out from the will. Furthermore, the 2016 will in which I was a beneficiary was very similar to previous wills written up, including that of my grandfather two decades previously. The 2019 will Leigh had presented was completely different. So purely on what the 2019 will didn't include, Leigh's claims seemed undermined. Throughout the whole ordeal, I don't believe Leigh was ever aware of the other properties that were owned by Maureen.

Another flaw in Leigh's claim came from the fact that none of the carers who looked after Maureen had ever heard of Leigh Voysey before. She had appeared out of nowhere. In her final years, with her declining health, Maureen had been looked after by several carers, and there was a book which all carers, and visitors, used to sign in when visiting Hill House. Unsurprisingly, Leigh Voysey's name had not appeared on the sign-in book on the evening in September 2019, when she claimed to have visited Maureen with the new 2019 will to sign. Nor was her name written as a visitor at any other point during the years she supposedly visited Maureen. The names of Leigh's witnesses were also absent. So not only had none of the carers who had regularly looked after Maureen ever heard of her, but Leigh and her witnesses hadn't appeared on the sign-in book which every visitor had to sign upon arrival at Hill House. Maureen was in poor health and bed-ridden by this time and wouldn't have been able to answer the door to Leigh, so this also raised a lot of suspicion (Maureen was so unwell she couldn't even hold a phone by this stage). Additionally, all visitors required a code to access the property before signing in, so how did she come by this code? Clearly, it was implausible that Leigh could have accessed the property.

Furthermore, it is worth mentioning that Maureen was in regular contact with some of the other beneficiaries in her final years. As already mentioned, I had nothing to do with Maureen, but some of the other beneficiaries were in regular contact and so would have been aware of the comings and goings, and also would have been informed of Maureen's general health. One beneficiary was in regular contact with Maureen's carers and was often made aware of any visitors. The beneficiaries and none of the carers had heard of Leigh Voysey before, and these carers wrote statements for our solicitors confirming this.

These issues were raised by our solicitors in their efforts to force Leigh Voysey to desist, but she was not to be deterred. Leigh argued that she remembered Hill House from her one shift as a carer to Maureen. She also claimed the gardener had been present at the time. This was a rather convenient witness as the gardener had since passed away. So, the only person who allegedly saw Leigh was now deceased. Added to this, Leigh claimed she arrived with her new will in the evening once everyone had left the property. The notion that the gardener would still be present at the property after dark on a late September evening was extremely unlikely. Having had a Saturday job working for a gardening company whilst studying for my A-levels, I knew work was never carried out after dark in the evenings, especially in late September. This was without taking into account the sign-in book at Hill House the gardener would have used that evening had he actually been present when Leigh Voysey stated.

Leigh's argument that Maureen hadn't wanted Hill House sold to developers was also something that was easily rebutted and another reason I believed she was lying. I felt this was just something Leigh had made up in an attempt to steal the estate. After all, she would have needed to have come up with *some* reason as to why the entire estate was being left to her. Prior to her passing, Maureen had been in contact with the solicitors and knew the land would be sold to developers. Maureen had even passed a comment that she didn't care what happened to the land once she died, and as well as our solicitors, we also had a developer who bought the land as a witness to these statements. Maureen had had developers looking at the land prior to her passing and they provided another witness for us. Leigh's claim that Maureen hadn't wanted the land sold was completely untrue. This point also highlights that Maureen had always used the solicitors when dealing with the estate and its future, always entrusting them in its management during her life and as an executor upon her death. Every year, Maureen had paid the solicitors what was almost equivalent to a storage and maintenance fee for previous wills, including the 2016 version. This further undermined Leigh's entire story.

As must be apparent by now, Maureen's health had been declining for a number of years and by September 2019, Maureen was physically and mentally deteriorating. She had suffered a stroke in June 2019 and was incapacitated. Carers had often commented that following her stroke, she had not been compos mentis (which is a legal term for not being in control of one's mind); Maureen often believed she was still headmistress at the Barn School. She certainly wasn't able to reason clearly at this point, so even if Leigh had visited Hill House, Maureen wasn't of a sound mind to willingly and knowingly draw up a new will. Thus, even if Leigh had been at Hill House, Maureen wouldn't have been in a capacity to agree to a new will being signed. Therefore, the possibility that the signing of the 2019 will could be legitimate was preposterous. I strongly believed the will had never been signed by Maureen in the first place, but this argument shows clearly that even if it had, Maureen would not have been able to do it willingly.

Despite these numerous factors undermining Leigh's story as well as the lack of any evidence, Leigh continued to persist in what I could only describe as a delusional claim. It was as if she thought the solicitors were going to bow to her demands and just hand over the estate to her without any evidence. Despite this, through the following months of 2021, I remained hopeful that there was some sort of misunderstanding and things would sort themselves out. But as the months progressed, Leigh persisted and continued to write letters claiming the estate was hers. I feared that this would have to be settled in court. Now, not only did we face a challenge to the estate but I faced the very real prospect of having to pay regular fees to the solicitors in defending the 2016 will and my inheritance. What made this particularly intolerable was that Leigh Voysey seemed to have no real argument or evidence, and yet we were still going to be forced to legally defend the estate. Even though she was clearly lying and deluded with no real evidence behind her, we would still have to go through the legal process.

This had a detrimental effect on my wife and myself. Not only did it put us in a difficult financial situation, it took a toll on our mental health. I couldn't help but think about the case, and frequently became angry and frustrated. I wished I had somehow had the foresight to see that this was going to happen so that I wouldn't have spent the inheritance and would have it available to afford the inevitable court case that was now becoming more of a possibility with every passing day. In truth, I knew there was no chance I could have seen this situation arising, but I couldn't help but blame myself. Additionally, my wife became anxious. What if Leigh Voysey ended up winning? What would happen to us? Even though Leigh's claims were ridiculous and we believed them to be completely untrue, these fears couldn't help but arise. Nothing seemed certain. My wife started to panic that we would have to pay back the money we had already spent and how on earth were we supposed to do that? Would we have to sell our house and relocate back to living with our parents? That was without worrying about the invoices we would soon face from the solicitors for payment of their legal fees. I knew the whole contest over the will was having a massive impact when my wife told me one day that she wished I'd never been given any inheritance. Our lives had been fine without it and we wouldn't now have this hassle and possible financial trouble. I couldn't help but agree with her.

As 2021 progressed, a possible court case loomed. Leigh Voysey continued to send letters claiming the estate was hers. Our solicitors kept urging her to desist, or if not, to make a claim against the estate, whilst highlighting the lack of evidence in her claim. Finally, after nearly six months of backwards and forwards correspondence, on 18 November 2021, Leigh Voysey officially served her claim; what I feared the most had become a reality and our solicitors now wanted us to select a barrister to represent us in our defence. We had until 16th December to finalise a defence for myself and the other beneficiaries. They sent over various CVs, with hourly rates costing from £300-£550, depending on the experience of the barrister. I now faced monthly payments to the solicitors for any work they carried out on our case. This was costly and I faced the very real prospect of paying hundreds of pounds a month on legal fees. Bearing in mind, I had spent all my inheritance on moving house so it wasn't money I had readily available. Added to this, I couldn't rely on money from the final instalment that had yet to be paid. As the estate was now being contested, the remaining inheritance I was due would be put on hold until the matter was resolved. I now faced a difficult financial situation with a mortgage and bills to pay alongside a now costly legal case. I was suddenly in a situation I wouldn't have imagined possible just a few months previously; I was financially worse off than I was before I received any inheritance. To give you an indication of the costs I was paying to the solicitors, I paid an invoice of £600 at the end of November 2021. I echoed my wife's sentiments once more in that I wished I had never even received the inheritance in the first place; it wasn't worth the stress and anxiety. The prospect of possibly having to sell the house gave me sleepless nights.

I think it's important to stress that I held and still hold no blame or any ill-feeling towards our solicitors; they were just doing their jobs and following the right processes. It was through no fault of theirs that I was in this scenario. I just want to highlight the difficult position I was now in personally as a consequence of this legal case.

Alongside the beneficiaries and with the advice of the solicitors, we decided to select the most experienced barrister to prepare our defence. If this was going to court, we wanted the best person for the job to represent our case, even if it did mean we would be paying higher fees. In January and February 2022, the beneficiaries and our solicitors held Zoom meetings to determine our next steps and to outline our defence. I won't bore you with the intricate details of our defence (you can find the main points of our defence using a simple internet search), but they were largely based on the reasons set out above: the testimony of the carers, developers and Maureen's incapacity at the time. Specific details such as the layout of the room in Hill House at the time of September 2019 and a forensic analysis of the 2019 will would be used as evidence to back up our defence.

By this point, I didn't want to put any further stress on myself so decided to try not to look at the ins and outs of our case and trust our defence team to do their jobs. I signed and approved what was required of me without dwelling further on the finer details. I wanted to try and put the issue to the back of my mind and carry on with my life. Leigh's claim had made 2021 a very difficult year.

This was without taking into consideration the COVID lockdowns that were ongoing at this time. I knew this whole debacle was taking a similar toll on the other beneficiaries when a comment was made about paying Leigh Voysey off to bring an end to the matter. This was quickly dismissed. Someone who we felt was clearly committing fraud in our eyes deserved nothing, and besides, if we did pay her, we felt it would lend validity to her case and make us look the guilty party. This suggestion was dropped and I only wanted to highlight it to emphasise just how desperate and frustrated we were by this time. We just wanted the matter resolved.

Thus, I began 2022 accepting that this would just have to be settled in court through a full trial, no matter how ridiculous I felt it all was. As our solicitors worked hard to prepare our defence, I accepted that they knew best and tried my best to put the ordeal to the back of my mind and get on with my life. Besides, the trial wouldn't be for a long time and there was no point in me getting wound up by it.

This could well have been the end of the story. But then, on 31st March 2022, I stumbled upon our case plastered across the front page of national newspapers. Things were about to take a dramatic twist.

PUBLICITY AND THE POLICE

MARCH-MAY 2022

Towards the end of March 2022, a procedural hearing had been scheduled for June. In the meantime, our solicitors had written to Leigh Voysey's witnesses in an attempt to press them to desist in their support. We weren't giving up on getting this resolved as quickly as possible. However, this failed to convince any of the witnesses in their support of Voysey, so any chance of bringing the matter to a premature end seemed out of the question. Both witnesses to the 2019 will stood by Leigh's claim. We were also advised that because Leigh Voysey had no assets and didn't own her own home, any possibility of recuperating legal costs we were incurring would be highly unlikely. In essence, if Leigh Voysey were to lose the court case, she wouldn't have to pay any costs and could just declare bankruptcy. It felt like she was going to get away with her claim scot-free, which seemed so unfair considering how much we were now having to pay to fight her allegations, particularly given the lack of evidence to support her claims.

However, by this point I had tried to put this all to the back of my mind and not dwell on it. I would just become angry and frustrated and I really wanted to carry on and enjoy my life despite it all weighing down on me. But it seemed that I wasn't going to have much success. On 31st March, as I was having my lunch and scrolling through the news as I usually did on a weekday, I stumbled upon a news article of our case. I was flabbergasted. It was one of those rare moments I was so shocked that I literally spat out my tea:

Former head girl, 42, is accused of faking old headmistress's will four months before she died aged 82 in bid to claim seven-bed £4.2m estate that was once the private school she attended.

How on earth had our case made it to the national news? Had someone leaked the case without our knowledge? As I scrolled through the article, I saw all the details of the case and our defence against Voysey. There were even pictures of Leigh Voysey as well as some of the other beneficiaries featured. I even spotted my name mentioned briefly in the article. I searched the internet, and to my shock found that it wasn't limited to just one news outlet; the case was featured on several national news websites and on more than one occasion, was the top article.

Immediately, I rang my parents in disbelief before contacting another beneficiary who was already aware of the news. Following my parents' advice, I didn't say anything to anyone else and ensured I kept a low profile. My parents warned me that journalists may soon attempt to contact me and if they did, to not respond: it could jeopardize the whole defence of our case if I spoke publicly. Thankfully, I wasn't put in that position: no one contacted me, although a few people I knew had seen the article and asked me questions about it. After all, my surname isn't the most common.

There were some positives I took from the publicity. All the headlines and articles seemed to suggest they didn't believe Leigh Voysey's story. For example, one headline read: *Ex-private school head girl faked the will of old headmistress in bid to claim her £4.2million estate.* It reassured me that if the journalists believed that she was lying, then surely a judge and jury would see through her as well. Added to this, the majority of the comments from the general public on the articles seemed to believe she was lying and trying to steal the money. This was without any of the articles mentioning a number of what I believe were critical facts that I felt would further discredit Leigh Voysey in the eyes of the public. None of the articles seemed to mention that Maureen had left a large portion of the estate to a number of charities. If the public knew this, it would surely make them even more sceptical of Leigh's claims. Also, some comments alluded to us as beneficiaries being greedy and driven by money. If they had known Maureen had in fact left a huge percentage to charity, they might not have felt so strongly.

Another detail the articles hadn't mentioned was that a significant portion of the inheritance had already been distributed to the beneficiaries. There wasn't any indication that Leigh Voysey had appeared out of nowhere more than a year after Maureen's death when the estate had already been largely distributed. Further to this, Leigh's claim of being too ill for over a year was an incredibly weak excuse. Her late arrival and justification for not coming forward certainly raised eyebrows for me and I feel the general public would also have raised a lot more questions if they had been made aware of this further information. Despite this, it was clear the public could see through Leigh without needing these extra details. It was gratifying for me to see the public's take on it. It reassured me that in the trial, the court would also see through her lies and find flaws in her story.

Some public comments mentioned that we should have followed the proper procedure to avoid a situation like this. Others commented on different countries' approaches which were far more efficient and avoided costly court cases such as ours. It annoyed me that people felt this way. We *had* done everything properly: there was nothing we could have done to avoid a situation such as this. This was the first time I began to clearly see a need for reform to the laws surrounding wills and probate in the UK. Like our case, I had previously seen countless articles popping up over the years involving inheritance disputes, and if laws weren't changed, ours certainly wouldn't be the last. Surely something could be done to stop this? I started to see this was a widespread issue that needed addressing.

I didn't know it at the time but the case going to national news ended up being a blessing in disguise. I now view it as the best thing that could have happened to us as it completely changed the direction of events. Soon after the news broke out, I received an email from my solicitors. Firstly, they acknowledged the media attention our case had received and suspected it came about as a result of journalists reading through pleadings (which are publicly available) in their search for interesting cases. That answered one of my questions.

What was more interesting was what developments occurred in the days and weeks after the news article broke. It brought forward a witness. This witness had seen the articles and contacted our barrister who had been named as representing us across the numerous articles. The witness was allegedly compelled to come forward because she was asked loads of questions by her son and imagined this situation happening to her family. This witness said that in May or June 2021, Leigh Voysey had approached her and claimed she was going to "win an estate". Leigh Voysey outlined her plans to this witness and asked her if she was prepared to stand up in court and say she witnessed the signing of this "new" 2019 will which Leigh had prepared following Maureen's death. The witness declined the offer. The witness said she believed Leigh Voysey to be a compulsive liar and was making it up (she suggested this was in keeping with Leigh's character) and so thought nothing more of it. It was only when the news articles broke at the end of March that this witness realised Leigh Voysey had actually followed through with her plans, and so, got in touch with our defence in order to support us and clear her own name.

Following the news articles being published, this witness further claimed that two of her colleagues had also mentioned that they had been approached by Leigh Voysey where she asked them to compare two signatures. Whose signatures these were or who they were meant to belong to was a mystery, but there was a strong suspicion this was related to the 2019 will that we believed Leigh Voysey was forging. What's more, the witness statement coincided with the time that Leigh Voysey first appeared, making this witness a reliable source. I believe Leigh only became aware of Maureen's passing when she saw Hill House on the market and drafted up her will at this time. This new witness coming forward was the first bit of good news in nearly a year since Leigh Voysey had first appeared. For the first time in a long while, I began to build a sense of hope and optimism that we could potentially avoid an expensive, full-blown court case. I didn't know who this witness was, but I was so grateful to her and wanted nothing more than to be able to say thank you in person. Her coming forward changed the whole direction of events. Moreover, her testimony validated my long-held beliefs: I was more convinced than ever that Leigh Voysey had never visited Hill House in 2019 and had indeed forged the will as I had always suspected.

Whilst initially ecstatic and hopeful, I was kept grounded by the experts; our solicitors advised that there would need to be another witness or some extra corroborative evidence in order to be able to effectively apply for summary judgement. Summary judgement was a much quicker and cheaper ruling than a full trial (around 10%

of the cost and resolved in a matter of weeks without needing a full court hearing). This was something we were now able to explore, but unless someone else was willing to step forward and give a statement, or we were able to find more supporting evidence, we would still have to prepare for a full trial. We were advised we needed more evidence as our application for summary judgement would likely end in failure if we tried at this point. The one witness statement alone was not enough as Leigh could argue that this person held a personal grudge. We needed another witness.

As a result of these developments, our solicitors once more contacted Leigh Voysey, informing her of what we now knew and urging her to drop her claim. We even agreed to not press any criminal charges or pursue her for any costs we had so far incurred if she dropped her claim and stepped aside. However, if she continued to press ahead at this stage, we would be contacting the police. Based on previous correspondence, I wasn't holding out much hope of Leigh Voysey desisting and I wasn't surprised to hear her response that she intended to continue on with her claim. What's more, I was told that Leigh had been blasé about the whole case going public on the news, even allegedly enjoying the media attention she was getting and boasting that she was now famous as a result. Even with our threat of reporting her to the police, Leigh appeared dismissive, even going so far as to dare us to as though she thought we wouldn't actually follow through with our threat (or whether the police would even be interested). Leigh even boasted that since the news article, she had also had witnesses come forwards, offering to help her. I believed she was lying about these so-called witnesses at the time and unsurprisingly they never surfaced. Leigh was clearly trying to call our bluff.

Despite the best efforts of our solicitors, no other witness was willing to come forward and testify publicly in our defence. Several people were contacted but none were prepared to come forward and publicly testify for us. I was frustrated but at the same time understood that many people wouldn't want the hassle of getting involved. Moreover, Leigh Voysey was still pressing ahead with her claim in spite of the revelations that had been brought forward as a result of the publicity. So, as supported by all the beneficiaries, the police were contacted. This had now escalated into a criminal case.

CONSPIRACY AND FRAUD

JUNE 2022-LATE 2022

Initially, getting the police involved wasn't as easy as we'd hoped or expected. The main beneficiary and executor of the estate tried contacting the fraud office police on our behalf numerous times, yet at first, they seemed uninterested at best. This was incredibly frustrating. Despite all this evidence and now a witness statement, the police appeared to be brushing our case off, even though we had a clear case of fraud going on. I was extremely disappointed to hear the authorities were not taking our reports seriously and it undermined my faith in the police. Now, I began to understand why Leigh had been so nonchalant about us calling the authorities. Could she have suspected the police wouldn't take an interest? It felt like every time there was hope, we were getting knocked back. Just as I was beginning to lose faith, finally a detective got in contact, taking an interest in our case and promising to get back to us. At last, the police were going to get involved and investigate Leigh Voysey.

Whilst all this was going on, we still had to progress as normal with the full trial for our civil case. We had some good news come through at the beginning of June 2022 when it emerged Leigh Voysey had failed in her claim to have access to documents relating to Maureen's 2016 will. Leigh wanted to access a log-book at Hill House to undermine the validity of the 2016 will. I believed Leigh Voysey wanted access to this to see what documents and evidence we might have that she could use. In court, Leigh Voysey alleged that she believed the 2016 will prepared by our solicitors was invalid and that it wasn't executed properly and believed that the witnesses did not attend the care home to witness the will. She sought disclosure of the log book from the care home to prove this. At the hearing, she advanced some far-fetched conspiracy theories about the involvement of the solicitors, the estate agents and the buyers of Hill House in the preparation of the will and sale of Hill House. Thankfully, her claim was dismissed in court as it had nothing to do with the 2019 will Leigh had come forward with. After all, the trial was about the 2019 will and its validity, not about disproving the 2016 will to which I was a beneficiary. In court, Leigh had allegedly further come up with some conspiracy theories regarding the solicitors and the sale of Hill House and used this as her reason for wanting access to the documents. I was given the impression that the court felt her theories were outlandish and she lost her claim. Thus, Leigh failed and was ordered to pay our court costs.

At this time, she also contested our request to have the 2019 will forensically analysed, which we wanted as part of our evidence. Forensic analysis of the will would have given us an indication of when the will was written based on the ink, as well as any discrepancies in signatures. At first Leigh

Voysey had agreed to it but quickly changed her mind. Like me, I think she was previously unaware of how far forensic analysis of writing could go and once she realised, panicked and then refused our request. This further validated my belief Leigh had forged the will in 2021 and I felt she knew she would be undermined by forensic analysis. However, Leigh Voysey's attempts to prevent us from analysing the will was also declined in court and we were given permission to progress with forensic analysis.

Soon after, Leigh lost a second case in court where she was pressing for a friend to represent her. Leigh claimed that she suffered from depression and anxiety and wasn't in good health to represent herself, and consequently wanted her friend to represent her. Furthermore, Leigh argued she had dyslexia and was unable to represent herself because of this. This friend she wanted standing for her was someone we suspected had been helping her behind the scenes and I was informed had studied law at one point, although was not currently a registered lawyer. Although entitled to a friend in court to quietly support her, we argued against her representing Leigh, using evidence that Leigh had been able to correspond perfectly fine through the numerous letters she had written to our solicitors over the previous year. Moreover, her evidence of having depression and anxiety was two to three years out of date.

This claim also failed because her friend was not officially a barrister and hadn't received her qualifications. Furthermore, it failed because our solicitors argued that this friend was not a suitable person to conduct litigation on her behalf as she had already led Leigh Voysey to make the first misplaced application that resulted in a cost order against her of nearly £4,000 and advanced the wild conspiracy theories against the solicitors and the 2016 will that did not advance Leigh Voysey's case. In summary, this friend had provided poor legal advice to Leigh already. The court sided with us and Leigh was also ordered to pay our costs for this. What's more, we would be able to use these failed claims as additional evidence to show how flawed Leigh's case was.

This was welcome news and I knew how desperate or deluded Leigh must be at this time to still persist in her attempts. Surely anyone with common sense could see that with the police now involved as well as losing initial claims in court would only serve to highlight the futility of the claim? That's what I reasoned anyway. But I felt Leigh was either so driven by greed or felt she had nothing to lose. Why else would she continue to pursue this claim which was becoming weaker every week and undermined by recent events? With the police now investigating, surely it was game over and it was in her best interests to step aside now before she ended up in a criminal court? However, by now, it was obvious we were not dealing with someone who viewed it this way. Added to this, she must have thought she would escape without punishment by not having to pay anything in the likely event she declared bankruptcy. I can only speculate as to whether Leigh had thought about this and whether this was playing a role in her stubbornness and refusal to withdraw.

So, it seemed that while she was still persisting with her claim, things were beginning to unravel for Leigh Voysey at this time and I still held out some form of hope that this could soon be brought to a close. By now, I had paid legal costs numbering in the several thousand alongside my usual household bills and mortgage. Added to this, I had a leak coming through my kitchen ceiling which was another added expense so I was still struggling financially. However, the possibility of a summary judgement was still there. We just needed some extra evidence. Furthermore, if Leigh Voysey failed to pay the costs of her two initial claims, then that would undermine her case even further. What was most comforting to me above all was the fact that the police were now investigating and believed there was a criminal case. Finally, it felt like we were being listened to. In the meantime, we just had to wait and see if there were any further developments.

Throughout the spring and summer of 2022, I was eagerly anticipating any update; we were waiting on the police and their initial investigations. However, we still had to prepare for the civil court case as usual, despite what was happening in the background with the criminal case. We had until the end of 2022 to prepare and submit final witness statements and disclosure to stick to the timetable for the trial. This was likely going to be held in the summer months of 2023. I was building hope that it would no longer need to get to this, but we had to prepare as if it was going to happen regardless. So, I prepared all the paperwork and documents the solicitors required of me, all the while hoping it would not be necessary.

We didn't have to wait too long to hear the results of the initial police interviews. Unsurprisingly, Leigh Voysey had stuck to her story regarding her 2019 will. One of her witnesses who had signed the will, Amber Collingwood, also supported the story. The third witness was more interesting. His name was Ben Mayes. After initially sticking to the story alongside Leigh and Amber, once pressed further by the police, he then admitted the whole thing was a lie. He denied meeting Maureen Renny or even ever visiting Hill House for that matter and had just gone along with Leigh and Amber in return for the promise of financial reward. Further to this, he even denied ever signing the will in the first place! This now led to the question that if he hadn't signed the will, who had? If Mayes was telling the truth, then someone had forged his signature on the 2019 will. I couldn't help but think back to our witness who claimed Leigh was comparing signatures. After the police interviews, we heard that several electronic devices were taken by the police whilst they conducted further investigations and we all awaited further news.

This was great, I thought. If one of Leigh's witnesses was now admitting it was all a fraud, then along with the testimony of the witness who came forward, surely, we now had enough evidence to avoid a full trial altogether and could apply for summary judgement? Yet again, my hopes were quickly dashed when it emerged the police were unable to release Ben Mayes' statement to us. They argued that if they did, it could jeopardise their criminal investigation and would make it harder to charge Leigh and her witnesses; Ben Mayes was particularly difficult as the release of his statement would make it more difficult to charge him for conspiracy to defraud. Not for the first time, my hopes of a speedy resolution were sunk once again. Despite more and more evidence emerging, we still wouldn't be able to apply for a summary judgement.

Despite this, there were some steps we could take to avoid further costs. With all these developments, we had a strong argument to apply for a stay in the proceedings. What this effectively meant was that we could postpone the timetable for the civil trial based on the events that were unfolding. What's more, the police offered to support us in our application to postpone developments by a few months. The police also informed us that they wanted to seek the release of the 2019 will from the court so they could forensically analyse it to see whether Ben Mayes was innocent or guilty of signing the will. As beneficiaries, we all agreed to support the police in their investigations, and the 2019 will was released to the police for analysis.

In the meantime, we once again wrote to Leigh Voysey urging her to withdraw her claim. This time, the letter was much more assertive, outlining what we knew had been said in the interviews (including Ben Mayes' statement) and giving her a number of days to desist. We agreed, once more, to not pursue her for any financial costs she had caused us up to this date if she accepted our terms in the timeframe given. If she refused or failed to reply within this time, we warned her that we would be seeking financial compensation when she lost her case, which we said was now inevitable in light of recent revelations. The court would also be shown a copy of this letter to outline that Leigh had been given plenty of opportunities to withdraw her claim, which would make it more likely they would agree and grant our desire for financial retribution.

We hoped that by sending her yet another offer to desist that she would finally submit. What's more, we also hoped that the revelation that we knew about the police interviews and the potential that she was unaware Ben Mayes had admitted it was fraud, might finally make her buckle and give in to the pressure. I felt this was an extremely reasonable offer. Even after all the evidence that had come out since March, we were still giving her a final chance to withdraw and walk away without us pursuing her for any costs she had incurred on us all over the past year. This was going to be our final offer. Leigh Voysey wasn't going to get any more chances. I thought this was extremely generous of us at this stage, given all that had emerged. Bearing in mind, I had by this time already paid thousands in legal costs because of Leigh's claim and apparent fraud.

The deadline came and went without any response from Leigh which was unusual, as up to now she had always been responsive. We took her silence as a refusal and the offer expired. Of course, this was disappointing but by now, I had learnt enough about Leigh's character to be surprised and I didn't take it too hard. In the meantime, our application to postpone the proceedings in our own civil trial was granted. We had managed to buy ourselves a couple of months. We needed the police to make a formal charge in time in order to put a long-term stay (postponement) on the trial; without a criminal charge, the court was unlikely to accept another postponement. Late 2022 became a race for us and I prayed that the police would be able to make a criminal charge in the limited time we had. It was now a race against time.

CHARGES AND POSTPONEMENT

LATE 2022-JUNE 2023

With the clock ticking, I found myself checking my emails nearly every day in the hope of an update. If the police decided to make a charge, it would mean we could potentially postpone the civil trial indefinitely. The biggest reason for the urgency at this stage was that it would save me a lot of money in legal costs if the trial could be put on hold. This could potentially save me hundreds, if not thousands of pounds which would be wasted money if the police subsequently made a criminal charge. We just needed the police to make a charge in the time the postponement had given us. If not, the court were unlikely to accept another postponement and we would have to continue paying costs in preparing for our trial regardless. The only way the court was going to accept a full postponement was if a criminal charge were to be made. But there was nothing I could do except wait for any update. I had to let the police do their work and the solicitors do theirs.

In the meantime, I did some investigating of my own through social media. I was intrigued to see if I could find anything myself through Leigh's online activity.

Leigh had a Facebook page which was publicly accessible and I recognised several photos which had appeared in the newspaper articles back in March 2022. Clearly, the journalists had done some investigative scouring of their own. In Leigh's biography, I was bemused to see she had written that her daughter is her life. I found that ironic considering her attempt at fraud was only going to have a negative impact on her child. What would happen to her daughter if Leigh was subsequently charged by the police?

There were some interesting things I found through my own internet searches. I found out that Amber Collingwood, one of the witnesses to the 2019 will, was a good friend of Leigh and appeared to be a drinking buddy of hers on nights out. Through comments left on each other's photos, I could instantly see they were friends and I believed they had obviously plotted the 2019 will together. For me, it also explained why Amber Collingwood was sticking to Leigh's story. Whereas Ben Mayes appeared more distant, I suspected Amber and Leigh had discussed their plans at length. Who knew what additional evidence the police might find in private messages between them?

Furthermore, on a public forum, I had also seen Leigh comment on a community post in Much Hadham by the new owners of Hill House. The post described some historical finds from Hill House and how excited they were to be the new owners of the old Barn School. In the comments section on Facebook, Leigh had left a comment asking the poster to direct message her. For what reason,

I could only speculate, but I knew it had something to do with the will she was forging. This post appeared soon after Hill House was sold, around the time we suspected Leigh was in the process of forging her new will. I believed she could well have been asking the owners for any photos or old items of Maureen's to try and gather evidence for her own claims. Obviously, this is just me speculating based on what I could find on social media, but why else would Leigh be contacting the owners of Hill House at this time? I want to highlight that in the subsequent time since my own investigation, these posts have disappeared from social media and I presume have been deleted.

These pieces of information I found from my own searches were interesting finds. If this was publicly available, I wondered what sorts of private messages and incriminating evidence the police might find in their investigations. Nevertheless, conducting my own searches kept my mind occupied as I waited for an official update.

Thankfully, as we entered into the early months of 2023, everything began to fall into place and we were able to get a full postponement of the civil trial. This was due to the efforts of our solicitors who worked extremely hard to make sure all the paperwork was done in time. For this, I was incredibly grateful and still am to this day.

It emerged in the preceding months that the forensic report came back from the 2019 will made by Voysey. In it, the expert concluded that the will *had* been signed by both Amber Collingwood and Ben Mayes and so, any suggestion Mayes wasn't involved was quashed. Following the first police interview, Ben Mayes had wanted to come in to speak to the police in what was hoped to be a voluntary confession. Voluntary interviews were arranged for Mayes to come in on two separate occasions. However, on both occasions he was due to appear at the station, he failed to show up and so this never materialised. It was hoped by voluntarily appearing at the police station, he would give a full account of what had happened and how the will was signed, addressing the fact of what he had previously said in his police interview: that he did not sign the 2019 will, despite the forensic reports now suggesting that he had. However, Mayes never came to the police station and thus never gave his voluntary interview.

Added to this, the forensic report into the 2019 will also suggested that that the will was not signed by Ben at the same time as Leigh Voysey and Amber Collingwood as there were indentations found on a document showing only Leigh Voysey and Amber Collingwood's handwriting. This in itself undermined the will's validity as for there to be a valid will, all three had to be present at the same time; the report suggested this was not the case.

Furthermore, I was informed that the police had then since conducted a second interview with Leigh Voysey and her two witnesses, Amber Collingwood and Ben Mayes. Although not informed of any details, we were told that in these interviews all three gave a mixture of responses and 'no comment' responses to some of the questions presented by the police, although Leigh and

Amber still maintained they had been present at Hill House for the signing of the 2019 will. As to what these questions were or what evidence was presented to them in the interview, we were not told. I had my theories as to what evidence might have been found. I reasoned that if they had investigated online messages, they may have found incriminating evidence that they had forged the 2019 will through online correspondence to one another. Regardless of what the evidence was, the Crown Prosecution Service charged all three with two offences: (1) fraud by false representation under the Fraud Act 2006 and (2) the making of a false instrument with the intent it be accepted as a genuine under the Forgery and Counterfeiting Act 1981.

This was welcome news for all of us. We could now apply for a long-term stay in proceedings until the criminal case was resolved, which would effectively save us wasting money on preparing for a case which was becoming more and more likely to never make it to full trial. The timeframe was incredibly tight, but our solicitors worked extremely hard to prepare the application and paperwork and thankfully submitted everything in time. The court accepted a long-term stay until the criminal case was resolved. What's more, Leigh Voysey even agreed to this so that she could focus on the criminal charges brought against her. Thus, there was nothing more to be done until the criminal trial was concluded.

Since this time, Leigh had paid up the court costs she was ordered to pay us. We suspected this came from her family and the friend who was supporting her. A comment had been made by Leigh after the court hearings where Leigh asked her friend to pay the costs as it was her idea to challenge us on these fronts. Thus, I feel Leigh agreed to the long-term stay of our civil court case as not only was she facing criminal charges but she had been forced to pay our court costs which totalled several thousand pounds. I couldn't help but feel Leigh knew the game was up. However, it was too late now. I had no sympathy after all the opportunities we had given her to withdraw.

With the civil trial now postponed, along with the other beneficiaries, we agreed with the solicitors to put our case on hold until the criminal trial was concluded. Effectively, our case was put into hibernation and the solicitors would carry out no further work on our case. This would save us incurring any further costs. The only further update came in April 2023 when the police asked us to provide details of the invoices and financial costs we had incurred as a result of Leigh Voysey's claim. This was going to be used to highlight the victim impact that Leigh's apparent fraud had caused to myself and the other beneficiaries. We all agreed to the sharing of these details and I felt very grateful to the police and the prosecution that they were taking into consideration the impact this had had on all of us as beneficiaries. I knew at the criminal trial the jury would hear of the financial impact Leigh Voysey had incurred on myself over the course of the last couple of years. I hoped they would understand the toll this had taken on me and my family.

With the civil case now on hold and the solicitors no longer conducting any work for us in the aim of saving us from paying any more money, everything went quiet. The only further update came in June 2023 when Leigh Voysey, Amber Collingwood and Ben Mayes entered their pleas at the crown court. All three of them pleaded not guilty and the criminal trial was scheduled for October 2024, well over a year further down the line. I wasn't surprised they had entered not guilty pleas based on their previous interviews. Had one of them pleaded guilty, it would have allowed us to have a procedural hearing and conclude our civil case before the criminal trial. Alas, this was not to be and so we would have to wait for the verdict of the criminal trial in 2024 before being able to proceed.

Despite this, I felt optimistic. Having watched lots of crime documentaries, I knew the police wouldn't have referred the matter to the Crown Prosecution Service unless they had substantial evidence and were confident of finding the defendants guilty. I didn't know what evidence they had, but I surmised it must be considerable enough for a criminal trial. I felt like even though it was a long way off, I didn't doubt the three would be found guilty. The events of the previous 12 months had revealed more and more flaws in Leigh's story and I knew she had nothing to go on. Even though I had incurred significant costs in defending our case over the past couple of years, I entered the summer of 2023 with a renewed sense of hope and optimism that justice would be served and everything would be sorted. As soon as the criminal case was concluded and they were found guilty, we would be able to have a procedural hearing and resolve the matter within weeks of the trial concluding. All I had to do now was wait. So, not for the first time, I once more tried to put the case to the back of my mind and carry on with my life. There was nothing more that could be done until October 2024. The best thing now was that I was no longer paying legal fees, and so for the first time in a couple of years, I felt financially like I was getting back on my feet. Things were beginning to stabilise once more in my life. As agreed, I received no further correspondence regarding our case as that would cost us and so I waited. Besides, there was little that needed to be reported anyway.

It would be more than 15 months until it once again came to the fore. In October 2024, the criminal trial began. Once more it would take centre stage and I would find the case in headline news once again. The story had reached its peak. Finally, we may get justice.

TRIAL AND SENTENCING

OCTOBER 2024

I started to type this chapter immediately after I received a text about the ongoing trial that would change everything. I wanted to get this down on paper as soon as I heard the news so I could convey the exact events and feelings on the day it happened.

When writing my story, I anticipated this chapter being a lengthy, roller-coaster of emotions, with some pretty intense twists and turns. It turned out to be exactly that, but not in the way I was expecting. As I was soon to find out, the events in this chapter were to be the most scandalous and revealing of the whole ordeal. When writing this chapter, I have written events as they happened (sometimes even on the same day) so you can experience how things unfolded for me as they occurred.

After June 2023, I decided to start writing this book as a way of processing everything that I had been through, as well as in preparation to share my story and attempt to change the law around probate and inheritance. Apart from that, I tried not to think about the case which, at the time, was more than a year away.

In early October 2024, we found out that the trial would begin on the 7th of the month at St Albans Crown Court.

It suddenly hit me. After months of silence, the end of this ordeal was nearing – whether the outcome was positive or not was yet to be seen!

I signed up to the CourtServe portal, a service which provided day-by-day updates on trials. Early on, I (and I believe other beneficiaries), were advised not to attend the trial in case the defendants argued that we influenced the defence. This was the advice given to all but one beneficiary, one of the executors of our will, who was due to give a witness statement at the trial.

In addition to this advice, I also stayed away due to my professional obligations. On a practical and economic sense, this trial was half-way across the country and I had work commitments. Being advised that the trial was likely to last up to 14 working days, it would be impossible for me to attend. So, I decided that I would wait until nearer to the end of the trial before planning to attend and hear the summary statements.

In the meantime, the only news I could glean was from the updates I would receive from those who could attend the trial, as well as what I could find on the daily court listings. Apart from this, there was very little I could do, and although I could see the light at the end of the tunnel, I was still very much in the dark. In no way did I want to jeopardise the trial with my presence so although I found the lack of news frustrating, I knew it would be for the long-term benefit. Little did I know that the trial would so suddenly be cut short.

On Tuesday 15th October, I was just about to have my lunch when I received "the text". My sister said she had been left a voicemail, saying there was "good news" from the trial, and she would call back straightaway. My heart skipped a beat. My immediate thought was, "someone has changed their plea". I ran this idea past my wife. "No," she said, "that is far too straightforward." After what felt like a lifetime dealing with the ordeal, I was inclined to agree. Way too easy. Why, all of a sudden, would someone change their plea after years of pleading "not guilty"? There even came a point where I started to question our defence and doubt my own views. Surely someone couldn't keep up a story for over three years if it wasn't true? Or maybe they could…

Half an hour went by. Nothing. I couldn't concentrate on my work, and took to pacing around the house, procrastinating with odd jobs. Then, my phone buzzed. I read the text out several times as I could not seem to grasp what I was reading. My wife did the same.

I was not expecting this. Not one, but all three defendants had changed their pleas to "guilty". Just one week into the trial. Ben and Amber pleaded guilty to the count of forgery and Leigh to both forgery and fraud. All three didn't take to the stand after the defence summarised their position. According to reports, all three of them had been in tears. What's more, I learnt that the judge was going for a custodial sentence for all three of them.

However, I still had so many questions. Why had they changed their plea? What evidence had been put forward at the trial, that convinced three persistent individuals to change their three-year long story? At this point I didn't know. I had my guesses, of course, but that is all they were – guesses. I had a feeling that technology and social media had a lot to answer for!

I later found out what had transpired during the five days the trial had lasted. After the first day of reaffirming their innocence, the presentation of the defence's evidence began. This included witness statements from those close to Maureen, including a number of her carers. They confirmed Maureen's deteriorating health during that period, as well as the routine and relationship with Maureen, indicating that they had never seen nor heard of the three defendants before. Following this, the individual who came forward after our story was released in the national papers gave evidence. They confirmed that Leigh Voysey had approached them, asking them if they wanted to sign the fraudulent will in exchange for a percentage of the inheritance. Further forensic evidence was also given, including a detailed forensic analysis of the "2019 will". It appeared that upon reflection of the evidence provided by the defence, Ben Mayes, followed shortly by Amber Collingwood, pleaded guilty. Subsequently, Leigh Voysey had no further option but to also plead guilty.

After dwelling on what had taken place in the trial and the feeling of confusion and bewilderment, a sense of relief finally rushed over me. I was in shock and emotionally drained. It had been nearly five years since Maureen had died and now it was all finally over. It took a long time to sink in.

Of course, I still had wait for the judge to pass their sentence before I could finally tell my story; I had to wait for the details of the trial to emerge. In the meantime, I was informed that the court wanted to take witness impact statements from all of us.

The next day (16th October), I learnt that the court had been adjourned and the three individuals would be sentenced on 5th December. Although initially disappointed that we would have to wait several more weeks until the sentencing, I was comforted by the fact that they had admitted their guilt, and subsequently the trial could not be prolonged by an appeal. I was also excited by the anticipation of attending the sentencing in person, which was only scheduled for one day. I don't know why, but the prospect of confronting the three individuals who had made my life hell for over three and a half years gave me a rush of adrenaline and satisfaction.

In the meantime, the police contacted me and asked me to write out a Victim Impact Statement (VPS). It was odd to think of myself as a "victim", especially when you read about others who have truly experienced emotional and/or physical trauma. However, I soon realised that I shouldn't downplay what I and my family had experienced. It was a crime, plain and simple, and we were on the receiving end. The VPS truly helped me see this as it gave me a chance to express how the ordeal of the previous few years had impacted my life.

I was also given the opportunity to be present and read out my statement to the court in person. I would finally be able to see the people who had ruined years of my life in person and tell them exactly what damage they had done to my life. I very quickly busied myself with writing down my statement. This is what I wrote and submitted:

By the age of 27, I found myself in a position that most people my age could only dream of. I never thought that by this age, I would be able to move into my forever-home and have a sense of financial stability. Not only have me and my wife worked and saved hard for most of our lives to achieve this, but the inheritance Maureen RENNY left me helped us to realise our dream before the age of 30.

Several months after moving into our dream home, shortly after receiving the second instalment of Maureen's inheritance, news came of VOYSEY, MAYES and COLLINGWOOD and the "2019 will".

This challenge sparked a level of anxiety in me that I have never experienced before in my life. The life that we had worked so hard to build was under threat of collapsing. Would we be expected to sell our home, built not just on the inheritance but our life savings? If so, the likelihood of having to quit our jobs and lives and relocate back to our parents seemed highly probable.

I had never felt so threatened by people I had never met or heard of before. We have always tried to live within our means but the sudden, unexpected threat of having to repay the inheritance on defending a court case left us feeling on the brink of financial ruin.

Not only was the unknown triggering my anxiety, but the financial implications of, what I now see as an unnecessary spend, on a civil case have exhausted my savings and has left me indebted to my parents and my in-laws. Although I am forever grateful to our lawyers and the court system, that is thousands of pounds I am unlikely to ever see again. I often found myself wishing I had never been left any inheritance in the first place.

I also felt a huge degree of guilt. My wife, who had not asked for any of this, was also feeling both the emotional and financial burden of the situation. She would be kept awake at night, worrying about the very real possibility of having to sell our house.

Furthermore, I had always intended to keep the news of my inheritance quiet, known to only immediate family. Not only was I shocked to see my name in the national press, but so were family, friends and even some of my clients. Although all hugely supportive, at the time I felt embarrassed and concerned for my anonymity.

So many negative thoughts were running through my mind, that the only way I could regain control was to record the events and the impact this was having on me. If a close friend of mine hadn't recommended I did this, I would dread to think how my mental health would have deteriorated. Keeping a journal of events was the only way of coping with the stress and pain of what I was going through.

VOYSEY, MAYES and COLLINGWOOD have put me and my family through an enormous amount of unnecessary emotional and financial stress. I will never get these 4 years back, and the feeling I have of what should have been a final gift from Maureen and my grandfather has now turned from gratitude to bitterness.

However, now they had changed their pleas to guilty, we still had to decide what needed to be done regarding the civil case. We wanted to bring the case to a quick close. What was the point of continuing a civil case and incurring further expense when Voysey, Mayes and Collingwood had already pleaded their guilt? Surely our court system was not so outdated and bureaucratic that the outcome of the criminal case did not significantly impact the civil case?

The solicitors advised that we continue with legal proceedings as planned. Despite pleading guilty, it still appeared that not only was the onus on us to progress with the civil case, but also the further expense. It seemed ridiculous that we would bear this burden despite the fact that all three parties had pleaded guilty. We had been in anxious anticipation and financial debt for nearly three years, and despite the fact we believed it was all over, the solicitors appeared reluctant to distribute the remainder of the estate to help relieve the unease. I could tell at this point that this wasn't the end of the drama.

It quickly emerged that Leigh Voysey had in fact been hiding a property throughout both the civil and criminal case, from the lawyers, police and courts. Throughout the whole ordeal, Voysey had led us to believe she owned no assets nor property. For this reason, our expectations were managed from the start: if she were found guilty, we would still have to cut our losses. This turned out to be a lie. We were alerted to the fact that she had put her flat on the market for auction, days before changing her plea to guilty. It seemed clear that she was now trying to sell her property and hide her assets as quickly as possible before her sentencing, in order to avoid paying for our legal expenses. Once more, it felt like Leigh Voysey was trying to cheat the system, lying to the authorities and trying to get away with fraudulent activity, even whilst appearing in court.

Time was of the essence. Initially, I was livid that she could be so brazen to act in this way and worried that she might actually get away with it. What could we do to stop it? If she sold the property quickly, it was possible that she could safeguard the money. However, as I thought more about it and how supportive, efficient and pro-active Hertfordshire Police had been throughout the criminal trial, I reassured myself that she would never be able to get away with it. Property would take weeks to sell which would give the authorities plenty of time to act. I was aware the court had powers which would allow them to place restrictions on her bank account and monitor the property. Hertfordshire Police had been outstanding in their support of us up until this point, so I reassured myself that they were experienced and qualified to deal with issues such as this. Sadly, I don't envisage this was the first time they had had to deal with this sort of activity.

Our solicitors still wanted us to take legal proceedings in light of these events, however, which would only add to the cost of the estate. It was estimated that we would be expected to pay a further £40,000 between us on top of what was already paid. It seemed a complete waste of money as the three had already changed their pleas to guilty. Why pay thousands of pounds more on a case that was practically over? The cost of this would probably never be recuperated from Voysey, Mayes and Collingwood. Even if we were to get financial compensation from them, it would likely never amount to what we had already paid in fighting this legal case. Therefore, despite the solicitors urging us to take legal proceedings, we decided that the legal fees were not justifiable and we would rather let the court and police do their job instead of spending any further money on a case which was drawing rapidly to a close.

Frustratingly, I and the other beneficiaries now found ourselves in a battle to commence proceedings to release the remainder of the inheritance which, if it were not for Voysey, I should have rightfully received more than three and a half years previously. Now Voysey, Mayes and Collingwood had pleaded guilty, there was now no further disputes of the 2016 will, and surely the remaining inheritance did not need to be put on hold. I became increasingly frustrated that releasing the remainder of the inheritance was marred with further red tape. It took a lot of pressure to release the remainder of the inheritance to us, but finally, the solicitors agreed.

As the weeks of October and November went by, I decided to look at Leigh Voysey's social media activity and saw she was selling all sorts of items online. Most of the items she was selling seemed like things that most people would either throw away or donate to charity shops. These were items I didn't expect many people would be prepared to pay for. In my opinion, it demonstrated how desperate Voysey was for money and had to relate to the court case and her admitting guilt. I also kept an eye on the property she was trying to sell and it appeared she had failed to sell it at auction as it was still listed. With just a couple of weeks before sentencing, the property vanished from the market completely. I was comforted by this fact.

In the meantime, the other beneficiaries and I decided to make an application for summary judgement with the aim of bringing the civil case to a close, while also trying to incur as little financial cost as possible. This was now possible to do, now the three individuals had pleaded their guilt. It would be far cheaper than a full civil trial. Once more, Hertfordshire Police were extremely helpful in supporting us with preparing the application. It seemed as if everything was finally drawing to a close. All that was left was to attend the sentencing in December.

*

The few weeks between the plea and the sentencing seemed like a blur. At first, it felt like an exhaustive amount of time, but it went quicker than expected. During this time, we were able to apply for a summary judgement which was successfully accepted, a hearing of which was organised for 4th December, just a day before the criminal sentencing. Conducted virtually, the Judge, Master Shuman, made the decision, without any hesitation, to grant probate in "solemn form" of the 2016 will, and ordered that Voysey pay £100,000 of our court costs within the next 14 days, with a remaining £97,000 at a later date. The judge concluded the hearing by adding "You have put up a forged will as being a true will. Something is out of the norm when a forged will is used to mount a claim in court." On a more amusing note, Voysey was frequently asked by the judge to remove her "love birds" which continued to twitter throughout the hearing – I feel like this request perfectly sums up the ridiculousness of the whole ordeal.

On 5th December, the day of sentencing finally arrived. The days preceding, I felt almost numb. I didn't know if I felt nervous or excited. My four hours' drive down to St Alban's seemed like a blank space of time that didn't actually happen. Before I knew it, I was parking up outside my sister's, whom I was staying with the night before.

I couldn't believe that it was coming to an end at last. Reading out my statement in person was far more emotional than I had anticipated and the chance to look these three criminals in the eyes was extremely satisfying. Finally, I was afforded the opportunity to have my say to the court. I was overwhelmed with a sense of anger and bitterness for what they had put me through and I wanted to make sure I looked all of them in the eyes as I read out my statement to the court.

I arrived at the court early doors, with the hearing being scheduled for 10am. The courtroom seemed foreboding as I took my seat at the witness stand. Taking a deep breath, I was called up to read out my witness statement. Despite it being a blur, I was certain that I held my own. I continued to look fixedly at the defendants' stand as I spoke. The atmosphere was so tense and still, that you could seemingly cut it with a knife. Sadly, mine and the defendants' eyes did not lock, as they continued to look down at the ground – either in guilt or defeat (I expect it was the latter).

All in all, the hearing lasted two hours, in addition to a brief interruption of the fire alarm which was set off by one of the defendant's friends. The time for sentencing finally came. Despite their solicitor clutching at straws to reduce their sentences, stating "good moral character", that they were "profoundly sorry" and that Voysey was "misguided", the judge was fully supportive of our side of the story. Despite being advised to do so, Collingwood had not brought a bag.

The Judge, Judge Jonathan Mann KC, said: 'You can call it forgery, you can call it fraud, but what it was was an attempt to steal £4.2million from someone who was no longer alive.' I think that this perfectly summed up the whole ordeal. Voysey was identified as the main instigator, who was accused of importuning both Collingwood and Mayes to take part in fraud. The Judge recognised their "commitment to the lie", not only signing a fraudulent document, but persisting with letters to solicitors and maintaining the case for over three years. I am grateful that Judge recognised the harm and physiological impact it has had on me and those involved.

I half anticipated a suspended sentence prior to 10am that morning, but as the hearing progressed, the comments by the judge and the atmosphere in the room made me optimistic of a custodial sentence. I was not wrong. Voysey was sentenced to six and a half years in prison, Collingwood received three years and Mayes received two and a half years.

Once the sentencing had been made, further details began to emerge. As part of the evidence against the defendants, "at-home" will kits were found in Voysey's home, as well as a script detailing what to say if asked about the "2019 will".

We had also learnt that Amber Collingwood had lost her job as an airport security guard that very morning.

When the judge reiterated the cost order against Voysey, their barrister contested that she had no assets so was unable to pay the cost order. To her barrister's shock,

Voysey's flat was brought to the table, and evidenced as an asset. The barrister's continued defence up until this point of Voysey's "good character" came back to bite them at this revelation. It was apparent Voysey had not only lied to the court, but also to her barrister. With this in mind, the judge was fully supportive of a cost order against them.

The judge questioned how this had been able to progress as far as it had based on no evidence – the same question that had been on my mind for the past several years.

The law had to change.

CHANGING THE LAW

My decision to write this account and tell my story has been driven by the hope that it can serve as an example of what I, and many others, believe is wrong with the probate system in the UK. I hope it can be a driving force for change. Although this was a particularly high-profile case, inheritance disputes are a regular occurrence in this country. You can often find a case in the news about a dispute over a will which has ended up in court. Ours was a particularly eventful and interesting case as I hope you have found from reading this. However, disputes over probate and inheritance are a frequent occurrence, and will continue to be an issue ending up in legal courts unless laws are changed around probate and the writing up of wills. The fact Leigh Voysey, someone with no profound evidence and little connection to Maureen, was still able to legally challenge us, underlines how the laws need to change drastically.

So, what can be done? I believe the main issues stem from home-made wills and the process of signing wills with witnesses. Anyone can purchase a home-made will as Leigh Voysey did and find any individual to act as witness for them. Clearly, this leaves the door wide-open for legal challenges. There needs to be more rigid laws regarding the signing of wills. Personally, I believe wills should only be valid if they are signed and witnessed by a solicitor or notary for it to be deemed binding. Whilst

I am not against the idea of home-made wills, I believe they should only be formally "rubber-stamped" once taken and signed by an approved solicitor. This means the signing and witnessing of the will should also be witnessed by an approved body to be officially declared as someone's will. Furthermore, I believe once this is done officially, there can be no way for a person to be able to legally challenge the will. The only way to change a will would be by going through a solicitor or notary once more, and this wouldn't be possible once the individual was deceased: their last will and testament would be the one signed at a solicitor or notary.

Another key issue which I believe needs to change is the length of time that probate can be challenged after it has been processed. In our case, Leigh Voysey emerged to challenge us more than a year after probate came through. The fact she was still able to take us through the legal process more than a year after probate had come through still baffles me. As you have discovered, the majority of the estate had already been distributed by the time Leigh Voysey came forward to challenge us, leaving me in a financially difficult situation. I feel that laws need to change surrounding the length of time that a person can come forward to make a legal challenge. I believe there should be a maximum time limit, possibly up to three months, for someone to challenge probate. Surely this could be easily implemented? Otherwise, what's to stop someone appearing years after probate has come through, long after the inheritance has been distributed? My story demonstrates how disruptive Leigh's late appearance and claims were. This could happen in future cases unless there are more rigid laws on the time limit for someone to make a claim against an estate.

In summary, I feel the system in the UK is too open and leaves things open to interpretation when it comes to the signing of wills and inheritance. Anyone could come forward and make a spurious claim against a will after the individual was deceased and be able to challenge it legally. Even if this doesn't result in changing the laws around probate, I hope there is at least some political debate regarding this and that a discussion around the ability to challenge a will is more rigorous. Leigh Voysey had very little to challenge us, yet she was still able to force us through the legal process which was financially and emotionally costly. I hope having read my story, you can see how easy it would be for someone to make a legal challenge. It could happen to you. Unless things change, ours certainly won't be the last case when it comes to inheritance and probate.

Printed in Great Britain
by Amazon